Sailing in Eccentric Circles

Ian Dear

Cartoons by Mike Peyton

Published by Nautical Books
an imprint of
A & C Black (Publishers) Ltd
35 Bedford Row, London WC1R 4JH

ISBN 0 7136 5940 8

A CIP catalogue record for this book
is available from the British Library

Typeset in Great Britain by
Latimer Trend & Company Ltd, Plymouth
Printed and bound in Great Britain by
J. W. Arrowsmith Ltd, Bristol

Contents

Introduction

The first two histories of that illustrious bastion of yachting the Royal Yacht Squadron, were called *Memorials.* Whether or not this was because the members of those days were already dead in their wicker chairs, they do reveal Victorian and Edwardian yachting as being both hilarious and eccentric. A third history, written by myself, was published recently; it not only showed that things have not changed that much at the Castle, but that there was an urgent necessity for an alternative look at our senior, though not our oldest, yacht club.

This deeply researched book, conducted with the help of a substantial number of pink gins, shows a lighter side to an institution which, for getting on for two centuries, has dominated the sport of yachting in Britain.

Peg Leg's white decks

One of the founding members of the Squadron, at first called simply The Yacht Club, was the Earl of Uxbridge, later the Marquess of Anglesey. The first meeting to inaugurate the new club was held on 1 June 1815, but the Earl was not present as he was leading a division of cavalry at Waterloo. It was during this famous battle that the Earl lost a vital part of himself. 'By God!' he exclaimed to the Duke of Wellington after a volley of French cannon shot had blasted the area, 'I have lost my leg!' The Duke's reply was brief: 'Have you, by God!'

The Marquess was extremely proud of the whiteness of the decks of his cutter *Pearl*, and when a guest left footmarks on it after a rain shower he instructed one of his crew to trail him and wipe them off as he walked.

Which Waterloo?

The sequel to the story of the Marquess losing his leg at Waterloo did not emerge for some decades. Some time during the 1890s the Duke's grandson, also a Squadron member, related to another member the story of his grandfather's leg. 'He lost it at Waterloo,' the Duke's grandson explained. 'Oh,' said his friend, 'on which platform?' The grandson was much disgusted by this ignorance of history and went across the room to complain about it to another friend of his. 'Do you know,' he said, 'when I told – – – that my grandfather had lost his leg at Waterloo, he asked on which platform it had happened!' His second friend looked sympathetic. 'The man's an idiot. As if it mattered which platform.'

Blow-by-blow account

Guess what the following was all about.

'The gallant Sir James Jordan, who was on board Mr Maxse's, had a narrow escape from a dreadful blow aimed at the back of his head by one of Mr Weld's men with a handspike as the two vessels were touching each other. He avoided the blow by ducking his head, and hitting out right and left à la Spring, floored the rascal with such tremendous violence that Captain Lyons told me afterwards he thought he was done for.'

An encounter during the Napoleonic Wars, or a meeting with pirates perhaps? No, just a yacht race in the Solent during 1826 when the *Arrow* collided with an opponent. The racing was very keen in those days—if keen is quite the right word.

Having a sting in her tail

The 110 ton cutter *Scorpion* was a typical racing yacht of the 1820s. Just in case she met an opponent like the *Arrow* during a race, she was well equipped with four brass cannon and an armoury of rifles, pistols and cutlasses.

The
fast-thinking boatbuilder

In the early days the few yachts which were built were modelled on Revenue cutters, and sometimes on the even faster smugglers' vessels which often evaded them. The Marquess of Anglesey, determined to have built the fastest yacht possible, asked whom he should approach to construct it. He was told that Philip Sainty of Wivenhoe was the best man for the job, as he not only built fast boats for carrying contraband but was a confirmed smuggler himself. The only trouble was that Sainty had been locked up in Springfield jail. This did not deter the Marquess at all and he persuaded the King to grant Sainty a free pardon. Sainty, however, was as wily as he was talented and refused to leave jail until his brother and brother-in-law were also freed, so the Marquess had to get all three out of jail before he could get his yacht built.

Permission to flog me granted, sir

The Squadron's first Commodore, Lord Yarborough, had a full-rigged ship as his yacht. *Falcon* was manned by a crew of 54 who had all signed a paper agreeing to be flogged if the need arose. Modern winch-grinders please note.

An early handicap race

Some of the early systems of handicapping devised by the club were bizarre. In 1831 the citizens of Cherbourg offered two cups to be raced for by the club's yachts, and it was decided to give a time allowance by starting the smallest yacht first and the largest last, an absurd arrangement over a course of only 24 miles. The French quite failed to understand the proceedings and after the race had finished were heard enquiring when it was about to begin.

The Commodore's role at the Battle of Navarino

Early members of the club thought of themselves as a kind of auxiliary squadron for the Royal Navy, a notion that existed for many years. In 1827 when the Royal Navy was fighting the battle of Navarino, who should turn up but the club Commodore in his yacht, determined to make himself useful. The yacht was apparently used as a despatch vessel, but the Admiral commanding the battle got so tired of the Commodore asking for missions that he sent him off with a message to the captain of a frigate most remote from the Admiral's flagship. The message read, 'Give his Lordship a good meal and he'll give you a better one in return.'

An unusual christening

The Marquess of Anglesey was a real old sea dog. He had his son Lord Alfred Paget christened by having him dunked head-first into the sea from the deck of his yacht, surely the most unusual method yet employed for introducing a baby to religion.

17

Social signalling

Signalling by flags between yachts was obviously an OK thing to do, for one of the first acts of the new club was to publish a signals book. The system was reworked over a number of years, until by 1831 the book was a large compendium which enabled members to signal messages like 'Have you any ladies on board?' to one another. Signals could also be sent ashore, and among those listed were demands for 'one hundred prawns' to be sent to the yacht concerned; there was also half a column on the 14 different types of wine which could be ordered.

Help!

At least one member found the signals book rather confusing. He had just concluded a rough passage to Torbay and the bowsprit of his yacht was broken and her deck in total disarray. When he was seen by a group of club yachts lying at anchor in the bay, in immaculate condition awaiting the start of the local regatta, a signal was raised asking for his club number. The distraught owner ran up the correct flags but in the wrong order, so that his message read 'Can I render you any assistance?', which caused great amusement among the other members.

Blackballing

It was only in Victorian times that blackballing became a common procedure. In its early days the club only blackballed on two occasions. Once was when the Duke of Buckingham failed to renew his subscription and was rejected on applying for re-election; and again when someone who owned a yacht that looked like a river barge was excluded. It was reported that this curious vessel, part of which was made of brick, had taken two months to sail from the Thames to Cowes, and members excluded her owner more as a joke than anything else.

The Rajah of Sarawak

One member who cruised successfully into a top job was Sir James Brooke, who in 1839 sailed to Sarawak in his 142 ton schooner *Royalist* and became its Rajah two years later. His even-handed administration made him widely admired by the natives, but his stringent operations against local pirates and head-hunters brought him into conflict with some members of the House of Commons. An enquiry was demanded and later granted, but Brooke was entirely vindicated. Irritated by the expense and stupidity of this political manoeuvre, Brooke remarked to Queen Victoria that he found it 'easier to govern 30,000 Malays than to manage a dozen of your Majesty's subjects.'

Pot roast

Another member, Ben Boyd, who cruised to far-away places, was not quite so lucky. He took his yacht *Wanderer* into the Pacific in the early 1850s, stopped off at the Solomon Islands and was eaten by the natives.

Cardigan's *bon mot*

The Earl of Cardigan was unpopular a long time before he led the Charge of the Light Brigade. In 1845 he was resoundingly blackballed when he was put up for membership, but was eventually allowed to join in 1849. He was a man described as having 'a strangely unconciliatory temper'. During the Crimean War he chose to live in luxury aboard his yacht instead of sharing the hardships of the battlefield with his men. Worse still, he knew almost nothing about yachting, and when asked by his skipper if he would like to take the helm, replied 'No thank you. I never take anything between meals.'

The Yankee Schooner

When the schooner *America* first arrived in the Solent in 1851 she was given the once-over by the old Marquess of Anglesey. 'If she's right then we're all wrong,' he pronounced. He then visited the yacht and added, 'I've learned one thing: I've been sailing my yacht stern foremost for the last twenty years.'

The Green Ensign

In the early days yacht clubs could fly either red, white or blue ensigns, just as the Royal Navy did. One Irish club decided on a different colour and in 1832 wrote to the Admiralty: 'A White Ensign has been granted to the Royal Yacht Club, a Red Ensign to the Royal Cork, a Blue Ensign to the Royal Northern, and as the only unoccupied national flag we have assumed the Green Ensign.' The Admiralty refused to allow this and the Irish club reluctantly agreed to use a White Ensign, not considering it any privilege but rather the reverse.

Annual
blackballing of candidates

By the time the Prince of Wales became a Squadron member in 1863 blackballing had become increasingly prevalent. The only real qualification for membership, one wag commented, was the possession of a steam launch and a collie dog. But others thought differently, and it became more and more difficult to become elected. 'The annual blackballing of candidates took place last Monday,' noted one commentator, 'When one out of seven was elected.' The difficulties a candidate faced to pass the ballot were underlined when one member was heard to comment that he 'always pilled a man whom he was tired of seeing and blackballed him if he did not know him.'

Just William

Eccentricity was not confined to club members. In Victorian times there was a club waiter called William who wore an old and shabby dress coat and had a habit of perpetually chewing something while on duty. He was also inclined to address strangers somewhat brusquely. On one occasion he spotted the Deputy-Master of Trinity House on the Platform. He had every right to be there as he was an honorary member, but William thought otherwise and asked him who he was and what he wanted. The Deputy-Master told him, and said he wanted some lunch.

'You can't have any here,' William retorted.

'But I thought we had the entree,' replied the perplexed man.

'You won't get no entrees here,' William said firmly.

Another story concerning William concerned the day when the Marquess of Ailsa was racing for the King of the Netherland's Cup in 1883. The day dawned grey with gale force winds and William warned anyone who would listen that they should not think of racing. The Marquess asked if he could take some cold pie from the dining room to eat while he was aboard, but William said that this was against the rules. Then he softened and said, 'Of course you shall have it, and I hope you will live to eat it.'

More blackballing: a favourite pastime

One journalist of the era passed the following comment on the club's habit of rejecting applicants: 'It is precisely this blackballing that makes the club to be so highly considered as it is, for in England the test of superiority is not looked for in the actual worth of a thing, but in the number of people who can be prevented from enjoying it.'

Certainly not, certainly not

When the Prince of Wales became Commodore, the Vice-Commodore, Lord Ormonde, took to chairing the Sailing Committee. He was an amiable man who had the unnerving habit—of which he was fully aware—of snapping 'certainly not, certainly not' to any suggestion, even before he had heard it properly. On one occasion the committee's youngest member asked whether a certain racing signal should be one gun or two. 'Certainly not, certainly not,' grunted Ormonde. 'Do you, sir, want the Squadron races to be run properly?' asked the youngest committee member in exasperation. 'Certainly not, certainly not,' Ormonde repeated, amidst roars of laughter including his own.

George Bentinck, MP

A great club character was George W. P. Bentinck, MP, who was a member from 1834 to his death in 1886. He was the epitome of just the sort of yachtsman of those days. He eschewed racing, loved the sea for its own sake, lived aboard his yacht and despised anyone who did not live aboard theirs, and never employed a captain. He liked nothing better than to be at sea, preferably in a storm of gigantic proportions. He was always delighted to take friends on these voyages, but his invitations were accepted with caution as he could never be induced to say where he was going or how long he was likely to be away, and much resented being asked. He was equally independent in the House of Commons and laid about both sides with complete impartiality. He once lectured the front benches of both parties by shaking his finger at them and saying, 'You know you have all ratted; the only difference between you is that some of you have ratted twice.'

The Pirate

Not all those who had been blackballed took it philosophically. During the 1860s there was one local inhabitant of the Solent—popularly known as 'The Pirate'—with a rakish black schooner of 150 tons which was armed with eight highly polished brass cannon. He found a proposer, but was duly blackballed and became obsessed by the belief that one member, Sir Percy Shelley, the son of the poet, was responsible for this humiliation. One summer's evening, while Shelley was dining in the club with a friend, the black schooner appeared in Cowes Roads and dropped anchor right off the Squadron Castle, the evening sun glinting on her brass cannon. The two men watched curiously as a small boat was lowered and rowed for the shore. It brought a message for Shelley. The Pirate demanded an apology, and if this was not forthcoming he would open fire on the Castle. Shelley refused, but his friend, who knew The Pirate well, begged him to reconsider as he knew it was not an idle threat. 'Even if he is hanged for doing it,' he told Shelley, 'that would be but small retribution for the damage such a bombardment might do. I therefore beg you, my dear Percy, to apologise in the cause of peace.' Reluctantly Shelley did so, and to everyone's great relief The Pirate dipped his ensign and sailed away.

(See front cover cartoon).

Let him who is without sin

During the Edwardian era a candidate who had already been blackballed three times reappeared on the list to be elected. On previous occasions he had been shunned because he had appeared in the divorce courts on more than one occasion, something most members pretended to abhor. On this occasion his sponsor dramatically declared: 'Let him who is without sin among you cast a blackball!' However, either the members present were especially virtuous, or perhaps they were just irritated by the remark, for the candidate then received more blackballs than he had on any previous occasion.

Sinbad the Sailor

Single-handed cruising was a pastime much enjoyed by one member, General Sterling, who joined in 1872. He owned an 18-ton cutter called *Chough*, and the extent of his cruises in her were always governed by the amount of corned beef carried aboard. He always started and finished at Cowes, and the object was to return to base just as he was eating the last of the beef. He was affectionately known as Sinbad the Sailor.

The reverend member

Another member during the 1870s who had a strong streak of adventure was the Rev. J. J. Curling. As a young man he paddled a canoe from Dover to Calais one afternoon and then returned with it on the night ferry. Later he volunteered to sail his yacht to Newfoundland to replace the Church ship which had sunk. His offer was accepted and Curling's 72-ton yawl *Lavrock* became the first—and only—Squadron yacht to be fitted with its own altar.

The
Prince of Wales' grocer

The German Emperor—who was, of course, an honorary member—felt a great rivalry with the Prince of Wales. He was very jealous of his uncle and despised his great friendship with the tea millionaire Thomas Lipton. When asked one day where the Prince was, the Emperor replied, 'They tell me he has gone boating with his grocer.'

Slow boat to Heligoland

One of the earliest ocean racing fixtures was the 300–mile Dover to Heligoland Race held every summer from 1897 onwards. Squadron members always raced, but their yachts were rarely built for speed. When one member entered with his old and extremely laggardly schooner, his son remarked, 'I'm sorry to see you going, we always had such good Christmases together.'

Brassey tacks

Lord Brassey was the first man to take a yacht around the world, and he was a typical Victorian member of the Squadron. He was an expert seaman who was not only the captain of his famous *Sunbeam* but a working member of the crew. On one occasion just after *Sunbeam* had been fitted with some studding-sail booms one of the crew began grumbling about how awkward it was handling them aloft. 'I wish the old – – – was 'ere 'isself,' he shouted to a mate. 'The old – – – is up here,' a voice shouted back, and the startled crew member turned to see his Lordship edging his way along the yard's footropes.

The right tack

The great passion of the Earl of Crawford—besides yachting—was astronomy. He was dining one clear summer night with a friend at the club, and during the meal he pointed out a particular heavenly body. 'Some day,' he remarked, 'that star may run into the earth.' His friend, who was a great racing man, replied: 'If it does, I hope to God we're on the starboard tack.'

Lord Lonsdale

The Earl of Lonsdale inherited his title from his elder brother. Perhaps because of his connection with the nefarious sport of boxing, members thought him something of a parvenu and it was decided that if he were ever proposed for membership he should be blackballed. Apparently, in those days it was not done to blackball admirals, and knowing this, Lonsdale turned up at Cowes flying an admiral's burgee from his masthead. When questioned as to his right to fly it, he replied that as Vice-Admiral of the Cumberland Coast, an honorary rank granted by the Monarch, he had every right. On hearing this all opposition to his election collapsed and he became a member in 1894. However, he had never had any right to this particular title, for though his brother held it it was not hereditary and in fact was bestowed by the Queen on another nobleman.

Soon after Lonsdale joined the club a large painting of all the most prominent members was commissioned from a well known artist. Lonsdale, obviously a pushy individual, ordered the painter to place him on the jetty in the foreground alongside the Kaiser and the Prince of Wales. Senior members were furious when they found out and the artist was ordered to remove Lonsdale immediately: he was repositioned, a much diminished figure, with other, less distinguished, members.

An unfortunate birthday party

Another member who came to an untimely—and some would say an entirely justified—end was Frank James, who roamed the world in his 479 ton auxiliary schooner *Lancashire Witch*. On 21 April 1890 he took a shooting party ashore in the Gulf of Guinea to celebrate his birthday with a day's elephant hunting. Unfortunately for both of them he winged a bad-tempered bull elephant. Enraged, the animal turned and charged James and speared him with one of its tusks, thus ensuring that Frank James had celebrated his last anniversary.

War of words

In 1895 when a Squadron member, Lord Dunraven, challenged for the America's Cup, the races developed into a bitter quarrel between his Lordship and the New York Yacht Club, which was partly about keeping the course clear of spectator craft. It so happened that the two countries were at diplomatic loggerheads over a boundary dispute, and a row over so prestigious a sporting event as the America's Cup did not improve matters. However, the tension was lessened when a London stockbroker with a sense of humour cabled his counterpart in New York that he hoped that, when war was declared, American excursion steamers would not get in the way of the British fleet. His counterpart promptly replied that in the interests of a fair fight he only hoped British warships were better than their yachts. 'All very funny,' Dunraven snarled later, 'but not funny to me.'

Dun racing

Though he lost his sense of humour during his 1895 America's Cup challenge, Lord Dunraven ordinarily possessed a sharp wit. He was a lot keener on yacht racing than most of his fellow members, an attitude he found so exasperating that he wrote a lampoon about it in the form of a parliamentary bill, and handed copies round to his friends. It is too long to quote in full, but the following paragraphs will give the reader its drift.

WHEREAS it appears that certain pestilent creations styled racing yachts infest these seas, and whereas it is expedient that they be speedily suppressed; and whereas objections to our rules have been made by certain ignorant and abandoned persons, to wit the owners of the said yachts; and whereas cruelty is practised on the crews of the said yachts by reason of the constant wetting of their feet; and whereas modern yachts are departing more and more from the lines adopted by the late lamented Noah, owner of the Ark;

Be it enacted with the advice and consent of the Committees, General and Sailing, in the Castle assembled, and by the authority of the same as follows:

1. In all races 'racing yachts' shall cross the line at the appointed time. 'Cruisers' may cross at any time of the day of the race. 'Bona fide cruisers' may cross at any time during the calendar month in which the race is sailed.

2. No vessel belonging to the RYS shall presume to sail at a dangerous rate of speed, namely a speed exceeding four nautical miles per hour, in ordinary races. In international matches she may exceed that speed (if she can) provided that the owner remains below, the sailing master be lashed to the wheel, and the crew be provided with adhesive plaster affixed to the seat of their trousers so as to guard against their sliding to leeward.

3. A yacht that will work under her headsails alone, and under her mainsail alone, is a racing vessel: a yacht which will generally wear and occasionally stay is a cruiser: a yacht which will neither stay nor wear under any combination of canvas or under any circumstances is a Bona Fide Cruiser.

Le Plus Select

By the close of the century the club had become so exclusive that one noble Frenchman who visited Cowes in his yacht in 1899 wrote that '*Le Club de Cowes, ou plus régulièrement le Le Royal-Yacht-Squadron, est le club le plus select, le plus aristocratique, le plus fermé, le plus intransigeant, non seulement d'Angleterre, mais du monde entier.*'

Entente Cordiale

When the French Northern Squadron, based at Brest, visited Cowes in August 1905, the Squadron threw a luncheon party for the French Ambassador and the more senior of the visiting naval officers. Later the same week the King reviewed the French ships and these exchanges caused a great deal of bonhomie. So much so that someone came up with the following quip:

'What is the *Entente Cordiale?*'

'It is the milk of human kindness which the English get from Brest and the French from Cowes.'

Damned women

The Squadron was founded by men for men, and the attitude of some of its members to lady guests, even during this century, has been somewhat equivocal. For example, when, in 1907, the Countess of Cardigan collapsed and died on that most hallowed of places, the Squadron lawn, one member was heard to remark, 'These damned women have no respect for the Squadron.'

Arming Squadron yachts

When the First World War was declared the owners of the club's larger steam yachts were asked to hand them over to the Admiralty for the duration. Most did so, though one was driven to write to the club's secretary: 'I have a letter from the Admiralty (marked 'secret', but of course you know all about it) which I suppose requires an answer about this arming question. What is any other yacht owner doing about it? As you know, arming a yacht of the size of *Medusa*, which steams only 11 knots or so, seems to me the most lunatic idea I have ever heard of in my life.'

For services rendered

Captain Rowe of Sir William Portal's yacht *Valdora* had previously been the mate on *Britannia*, and a very good one. When he left to take up his new job the Prince of Wales gave him a watch. Rowe was inordinately proud of this timepiece, and one day he showed it to Field-Marshal Sir Henry Wilson who had had an extremely distinguished Army career during the First World War before he was made a member in 1920.

'Whatever induced the Prince of Wales to give you that beautiful watch?' the Field-Marshal enquired.

'Services rendered, Sir Henry.'

'Nobody ever gave me a watch, or anything else, Captain.'

'Maybe you ain't done any services, Sir Henry,' was the prompt reply.

Ignorance is bliss

Mention of Sir William Portal reminds me of a story which shows that a candidate for the Squadron did not always have to be a proven yachtsman: indeed in Victorian times candidates would often buy a yacht before they were proposed and sell it once they had been elected. Sir William did at least keep his, though he apparently knew not the first thing about it and would leave the entire running of the vessel to his professional skipper, who made sure nothing too strenuous was undertaken. However, once, when dared to by one of his guests, Sir William did issue an instruction. 'Hoist the mainsail,' he ordered. As *Valdora* was at anchor at the time, the skipper was doubly amazed but did what he was told.

The best story of ignorance being bliss was told by Anthony Heckstall-Smith in his book *Sacred Cowes*. No one is certain that it alludes to Sir

William, but informed guesses reckon it must have been him. Owner and guest were being taken out to his yacht by his skipper, when Sir William began to take a lively interest in other yachts anchored nearby.

'That's *Shamrock* over there, isn't it?' he asked his skipper.

'Yes, that's her, Sir William.'

'And that's *White Heather* just astern of her, am I right?'

'That's right, Sir William.'

Sir William was by now quite carried away by his success. 'But I'm damned if I can recognise the other white cutter, which is she?'

His skipper seemed stricken by deafness, for he did not reply.

Sir William repeated his question. 'What's her name then?'

His skipper sucked his teeth and his face twitched. Sir William turned to his guest and laughed. 'The old boy's getting deaf.' He raised his voice and said, 'I said, who owns the other white cutter?'

The skipper could barely disguise his anguish. 'You do, Sir William.'

Rosa Lewis

As the 20th century progressed it came to be accepted that women were not going to allow themselves to be confined to having tea on the lawn. They wanted to sail too, but as there was nowhere for them to change in the Castle it was decided to negotiate the lease of a small building at the bottom of the garden of Rosa Lewis' house, positioned opposite. Rosa, intimate of King Edward VII, owner of the Cavendish Hotel, model for Lottie Crump in Evelyn Waugh's novel *Vile Bodies*, was a friend of nearly everyone but not the sort of person the Squadron allowed into its hallowed grounds. 'While they won't 'ave me on their old lawn,' she commented bitterly when negotiations for the proposed ladies' annexe were on the verge of breaking down, 'I 'ave to let their lady friends into my garden to piddle.'

The excitement of the start

Mr Herbert Weld, who was elected to the Squadron in 1924, owned the Big Class cutter *Lulworth*, which he raced very successfully. Or to be more accurate, his crew raced very successfully, for Weld, though he was on board, usually took scant interest in what was going on. The papers were always delivered to *Lulworth* about half an hour before the race was due to start: Weld would then go below with a copy of *The Times* tucked under his arm and would not reappear until the race was well under way. 'Hullo!' he would say, casually looking round him. 'We've started!' Such detachment from the excitement of the start caused astonishment to all who witnessed it.

An expensive experiment

Between the wars, racing in the small classes became quite popular among members. One of them, Colonel Moore-Brabazon, later Lord Brabazon of Tara, raced in the Redwing class. He did not consider himself much of a helmsman—he ranked himself as the equivalent of a golfer with an eight handicap—but he knew a thing or two about aerodynamics. The Redwings had a standard hull but were allowed any rig so long as the sail area did not exceed 200 square feet. For one of the country's foremost aeronautical experts this presented something of a challenge, and Moore-Brabazon was determined to make sure that what he lacked in skill would be made up for by the sheer speed of his boat. He was also convinced that the ordinary rig of a foresail and mainsail hoisted on a single stayed mast was about as up to date as the Wright Brothers' monoplane. He started by

trying a streamlined mast with one sail before fitting two masts with one sail between them. Later he tried the Lungstrom rig, and then a Flettner rotating cylinder 'mast' before alighting on his *pièce de résistance*, an auto-gyro. This seemed to him the most efficient way of all of exploiting any wind, and an engineer friend ran him up one which measured the equivalent of only 35 square feet in sail area against the 200 allowed. It worked well at first, except great care had to be taken that the crew's head was not chopped off by the blades, and he was delighted to be handling what was the first boat ever to sail without either sheets or shrouds of any kind. In winds of around 20 knots he achieved astonishing speeds, and he must have thought he was onto a winner when he entered her for the Redwing races in Cowes Week. Sadly, however, no sooner had he moored among a lot of other small keelboats off Cowes than one of his crew accidentally let the rotor go. There was a good breeze blowing and nothing could stop the Redwing taking off into the other boats: the rotor blades, revolving at high speed, chewed one boat to pieces before disintegrating. 'A very sad ending to an expensive but amusing experiment,' Moore-Brabazon commented ruthfully.

The Hon. Ernest Guinness

Unlike many members of the Squadron, the Hon. Ernest Guinness was very keen on moving fast across the water and after the First World War he acquired an ex-naval triple engined, high-speed motorboat. This moved at a fair lick but not fast enough for Guinness, and he asked the famous yacht designers Camper & Nicholson to add a fourth engine. This proved impossible to fit, at least in the position where an engine is normally placed, but when Guinness insisted that something had to be done the problem was solved by bolting an aero-engine on deck which drove a propeller. It only increased the boat's speed by about three knots, but Guinness was delighted and, as can be imagined, she caused quite a stir at Cowes Week.

Later Guinness owned a 303-ton auxiliary ketch called *Fantome*, of which he was so fond that when he decided he needed a larger yacht he had her lengthened by 33 feet instead of selling her. This entailed virtually cutting her in half and when this had been done it was found that parts of her were rotten. Charles Nicholson of Camper & Nicholson advised Guinness not to proceed, but despite the costs involved Guinness insisted that the job be finished, and when it was done confided to Nicholson that he had spent his honeymoon in her and would not part with her at any price. Her engines exhausted in a most unusual manner—up the mizzen mast. But this tended to be awkward as guests were often covered with smuts, so Guinness had an exhaust pipe made of flexible metal which was trailed overboard when the engine was running. It looked not unlike a sea serpent and was coiled on deck when not in use.

Mystery tours

Like some earlier members such as George Bentinck, Urban Broughton did not much like being tied down by itineraries. He voyaged far and wide during the inter-war period in his beautiful 1421-ton steam yacht *Sapphire*, whose mailbox was inscribed 'Do not ask when the post goes, you know as much about it as we do.'

Tiggy

In 1927 Sir Richard Williams Bulkeley, 'Tiggy' to his friends, became Commodore. He owned tracts of land in Wales, where he lived. He was walking down the High Street of the town of Beaumaris one day and taking a good look at things as he was wont to do, when he was spotted by some holiday-makers. 'Look at 'im,' said one of them, 'you'd think the 'ole place belonged to 'im.' This was overheard by the Commodore, as it was probably meant to be. 'As a matter of fact,' the Commodore said to them, 'as a matter of fact, it does,' which retort apparently went down extremely well with all concerned.

An inflation-ridden lunch

Not all members, of course, owned grand yachts. General Jack Seely, later Lord Mottistone, loved cruising in his small 14-ton cutter *Isme II*. She had an unusually high aspect-ratio rig, and he once described her as being very like the King's *Britannia* viewed through the wrong end of a telescope. In 1923 he took her to Hamburg, and was unlucky enough to arrive the very day that the German mark finally collapsed. He went ashore for lunch, at which he ordered a bottle of hock: this cost 100,000 marks, which by that time of the day was about 10 shillings. It tasted very good and he was just draining the last of it from his glass when the restaurant manager approached and said the bottle was now going to cost 250,000 marks. Seely remarked that though the wine was excellent, a 150 per cent rise in less than two hours seemed somewhat unreasonable, and a compromise figure was agreed upon. During that fatal day the mark fell from 100,000 to the pound to 500,000.

Looks like Spain to me, sir

A prominent member in the early decades of this century was Bendor, the Second Duke of Westminster. A Victorian who lived well beyond his time, Bendor loved yachting in the grand style but could not abide itineraries. Just for the hell of it, he would tell his captain in the middle of the night to alter course to quite a different destination from the one his guests supposed they were approaching. Sir Sacheverell Sitwell, a frequent guest of Bendor's, firmly believed that members of the crew were always instructed to say, 'Looks like Spain to me, sir,' when asked where they were, whether it was or not.

Flying Cloud's decor

The amazing Bendor had an eccentric taste in yachts. The interior of his 400 foot, four-masted schooner *Flying Cloud* was designed by Detmar Blow, the architect who was responsible for much of the Duke's Grosvenor Estate. The result was, as the Duke's wife commented, 'almost too odd to be believed in', for *Flying Cloud* below looked more like a house built in what might be called a neo-Queen Anne style than a yacht.

Beach the bitch

Bendor's other yacht *Cutty Sark* was hardly less remarkable. She was a converted First World War destroyer, the engines of which had all been repositioned on to the port side so that her passengers could walk the length of the ship below decks. The trouble with *Cutty Sark* was that she rolled abominably. On one occasion Bendor had had enough of the corkscrew motion and ordered his captain to return to port. When the captain said that it was not possible, Bendor snapped 'Well, beach the bitch.'

It was Bendor who was immortalized in Noel Coward's play *Private Lives*, which was set on the Riviera. 'What yacht is that?' one of the characters asks in the first act. 'The Duke of Westminster's, I expect,' comes the prompt reply: 'It always is.'

Queen Mary's thoughts on sailing

King George V enjoyed yachting to about the same degree that his wife, Queen Mary, hated it. During one race when she was aboard the jib-topsail flew loose and in the ensuing pandemonium the King told his sailing master to send someone below to see how the Queen was bearing up. One of the hands dived down the companionway and returned a few moments later to find the King facing him. 'Well, how is Her Majesty?' the King asked. The man pulled off his sou'wester and scratched his head. 'Well, what did she say? Speak up,' the King commanded. 'Her Majesty said— "Never again, she's – – – if she will",' the crewman stammered, much to the King's delight. She never did, either.

A floating palace

Between the wars quite a number of members besides the amazing Bendor indulged in unusual yachts. Lord Moyne felt he needed a really roomy vessel in which to venture far afield and settled on converting one of the Newhaven–Dieppe ferries. When her captain ran her onto a rock off Galway, he bought the other ferry and turned her into a floating palace which included eight staterooms, each with its own bathroom, and a swimming pool on the weather deck.

'A' for Adultery

In the 1930s the largest racing cutters, including the King's *Britannia*, were converted to conform to parts of the J Class of the American Universal Rule. When King George first saw the letter J on the mainsail of one of these yachts he asked what it stood for. 'It should have been "A",' he said, with a flicker of a smile, after hearing the explanation. 'Why, sir?' asked his informant. '"A" for Adultery,' the King chuckled. 'Because with the exception of old Davis, I'm the only owner in the class who still has his original wife!'

Ancient privilege

One of the Squadron's best known sportsmen was Sir Claude Champion de Crespigny, who died in 1935 aged 88. In his younger days he had been a reckless steeplechaser; he swam the rapids at Assuan; he crossed the North Sea in a balloon; and in his old age he took to bathing off the Squadron steps with his wife. These dips in the sea subsequently inspired a Bateman cartoon, for they were flouting the conventions of the day. However, when one indignant member asked the Commodore what he would say if asked for a ruling on the matter, the Commodore wisely replied: 'I shall say that this is a privilege reserved for members of 80 year of age and over.'

Bloodhound

Ikey Bell was an English-educated American who, despite a hunting injury, enjoyed yachting. In 1936 he built the famous ocean racer *Bloodhound*, a 34-tonner later owned by the Queen and the Duke of Edinburgh and by today's standards a fair-sized yacht. In the same year he was made an honorary member of the Squadron, and the next season he took her to Cowes and anchored her in the Roads between a large schooner and an even larger motor yacht. In the Castle he was spotted as being a new member by one of the Flag Officers, who by way of welcome asked if he was staying in the club. Bell shook his head and replied that he was sleeping aboard his yacht, and pointed in *Bloodhound*'s direction.

'Ah, the motor yacht.'

Bell shook his head.

'Oh, the schooner, then?'

Again Bell shook his head.

The Flag Officer looked puzzled and then amazed. 'What, not on that little blue yawl?'

Bell nodded.

'Good heavens, you don't sleep on that do you?'

The high-hat club

The Squadron has always caused some bewilderment among foreigners, particularly Americans. During the period of Prohibition in the United States, the wife of a visiting American yachtsman wanted to know who owned which yacht anchored in Cowes Road.

'Who owns that one over there?'

Ernest Guinness, she was told.

'The same guy that makes the Guinness?'

'That's right,' said her host.

'And that cute little black steam yacht?'

'That belongs to Richard Hennessy.'

'Hennessy's brandy?'

'That's it.'

'And what about that big white ketch?'

'That belongs to John Gretton. He makes a beer called Bass,' she was told.

'But they're all flying the White Ensign,' she said incredulously. 'Does that mean they are all members?'

'It does.'

'They all make hooch yet they're all members of the Squadron?'

'That's right.'

The lady laughed. 'No kidding! And they told me it was a high-hat club!'

Fore!

King George V did not pass on his love of sailing to his eldest son. On the one occasion when the future King Edward VIII was taken aboard *Britannia* he found the whole business too slow for words and spent the afternoon driving golf balls off the counter.

The pantry election

One of William's successors was Frederick, who ruled the Squadron kitchens with a firm hand both before and after the Second World War. He was, as his obituary put it, 'a Victorian by birth and by inclination.' When asked what he thought of the postwar election of one rather flamboyant but popular character, he replied darkly: 'If the election had been held in the pantry, sir, the result would have been very different.'

The dirt-track rider

There's a good story about the election of Sir Max Aitken which he often told himself. Two elderly members were heard mulling over the list of candidates when Aitken's name came up.

'Who's this fellow Aitken, then?'
'A Battle of Britain fighter ace. He's a pilot.'
'Good God,' muttered the first member, 'a pilot?'
'That's right.'
Silence ensued while the member digested this unpalatable piece of news. Then he spluttered, 'We'll be letting in dirt-track riders next.'

The Cretan cretin

During the 1930s one member, Harold Hall, raced 8 Metres with great success, but after the war he purchased a 200-ton twin-screw, diesel engined trawler which he called *Manahine*, and turned to marine biology as a pastime. In 1949 he went to the Gulf of Aqaba via the Suez Canal and encountered a less than competent pilot to guide them through it. 'The pilot, a little Cretan, gave us no confidence', Hall wrote in his diary. 'He had only one method. Full speed ahead or full astern. Met the southbound convoy after about two hours. He went past the first ship, a huge tanker, at full speed. *Manahine* was steering badly for some reason. The skipper and I were terrified. He did slow down for the succeeding ships but put years on us both. Did arrive at Port Said in one piece without ramming another ship or taking a bit out of the Canal. On arrival we went full astern both, into his berth, which ended in a stone wall. A horrid little bastard and we were delighted to see the last of him. He seemed to speak no known language.'

Unsuitable for cultivation

In 1940 one member, Lord Dorchester, had the temerity to suggest that the Squadron lawn be dug up and planted with vegetables. This astonishing suggestion perhaps originated from the grievance his Lordship felt at having to continue to pay his full subscription when he was unable to use the club because he was serving in the Army. As it happened, the local Agricultural Committee turned up their collective noses at the suggestion and deemed the lawn not suitable for cultivation. Later the subscription fees were reduced to £1 for the duration of the war.

The spy

Not all members raced just for pleasure. When Michael Mason took part in the 1937 Round Gotland Race, which he won, he and his crew did a bit of spying on the way. As they sailed round the course they took careful note of all the German fortifications and sent detailed descriptions of them to the Admiralty when they returned to England. Before war broke out and during the first years of it, Mason was employed as a spy. 'His unique combination of seamanship, linguistic ability, physical and mental stamina, accuracy with his revolver', as his obituary in *The Times* put it, made him a very useful member of that profession. Later in the war the Gestapo, much to his amusement, put a price of £10,000 on his head.

Lord Louis Mountbatten

Before he was eventually elected by acclamation, Lord Mountbatten was blackballed twice. No-one ever knows the reason why someone is blackballed, but the rumours flew thick and fast. That dashing Dickie liked to drive speedboats too fast through the roads was one, but probably the real reason was Lady Mountbatten who favoured rather outré swimming costumes which she was not at all shy of displaying. Also a headline in an American newspaper—'A Royal Spanking for Gay Lady Mountbatten' above a story about how Queen Mary had been much displeased at hearing that Lady M had danced the Charleston with Fred Astaire—might have had some truth in it, but perhaps not.

Courthauld's bloomers

On his first visit to the Castle after being elected to the Squadron, poor Augustine Courthauld, a member of the enormously rich textile family, committed a whole series of outrageous social gaffes. He came ashore from his yacht *Duet* in a blue reefer jacket and white flannels and thought he was pretty nattily dressed. Once in the grounds, however, he found everyone else wearing grey trousers. Worse was to come, for he had committed the appalling outrage of wearing a beret onto which he had attached the Squadron cap badge, and he had to be hurried to his proposer's room to have a spare yachting cap rammed on his head. It proved to be three sizes too small. Even more heinous was his crime in telling his wife to wait for him on the Platform while he made a telephone call. He returned to find the stewards 'white to the gills', as he put it, for she was the first woman to have got onto it for nearly a century. The final humiliation came when the Commodore had Courthaulds' four boys turned off the lawn as they were under eighteen, but later Courthauld got his own back by having the rules changed. Amazingly, Courthauld decided to remain a member and later founded a trust for teaching the young to sail in *Duet*.

Another social gaffe

No sooner had the rules been changed to allow the children of members on the lawn than another gaffe was revealed. The sons of one member, who owned a top-class ocean racer, had entered the hallowed ground wearing sweaters with the name of their father's yacht embroidered across the chest. This was definitely *infra dig* as in those days only paid hands wore such sweaters, and the children were asked to leave.

Red socks

Dress was in fact a matter of great importance in those early post-war years. Woe betide anyone who was caught wearing red socks (someone was) or worse still none at all.

A stickler for etiquette

Sir Ralph was determined to preserve the niceties of the pre-war days. So determined, that when a guest aboard Gore's ex-12 Metre *Tomahawk* decided to help himself to a glass of water, Gore motioned to him to remain seated. The galley's water tap was next to them, but instead of pouring the water himself Gore rang a bell. This summoned the one paid hand aboard who was ordered— much to the guest's embarrassment—to fill a glass and put it before him.

Pull-through's remarkable feat

Major Bolitho—he possessed the nickname 'Pull-through' as he was as long and as thin as the cord used by soldiers to clean their rifles—was a long-standing member of the Squadron and a keen afficionado of the 12 Metre class. An expert helmsman, he was almost certainly the only man ever to sail one of them backwards. He performed this remarkable feat when he found himself among the Ecrehous, a group of rocky islets near Jersey where the tide rips through at incredible speed. 'Pull-through' judged that he would have more control over his yacht *Morwenna* if he sailed at a slower speed than the current was carrying him. So he aimed the 12 Metre's bows in the opposite direction to where he wanted to go and, with the wind abeam, sailed steadily stern-first through the dangerous outcrops.

A case of mistaken identity

Perhaps some of the stories about the Squadron are apocryphal, but this one really did happen. The yachting correspondent of *The Times*, John Scott Hughes, was asked in the late 1940s to dine at the Castle with the then Commodore, Sir Philip Hunloke. The place seemed empty but then Scott Hughes spotted a member by a table in one of the corners, idly skipping through some magazines. Once in the dining room this member went to a remote table and started eating in total silence. At first Scott Hughes refrained from asking his host about this 'slight, elderly, inconspicuous figure, not to be readily otherwise described', but when the man had seemed literally to tiptoe out of the room after his meal, his curiosity got the better of him.

'Who was that?' he asked the Commodore.

'Eh? Who? Oh, some dam' feller. We elected him thinking he was his brother.'

The nicest
club in the world

Scott Hughes had no illusions about the Castle and its members during his era, as the following story he wrote shows.

'Once inside it is incomparably the nicest club in the world. I say, once inside . . .

'When I was living in London some years ago I was asked whether on behalf of a foreign yachtsman I would assist in taking to Cowes a 6 Metre yacht which was entered for the Cowes Week regatta. The boat had been unloaded at Southampton, where she was waiting with two or three amateur members of the crew.

'I daresay we were not all of us in the best of good humour when we reached Cowes—through my fault we had stuck in the mud for ten minutes or so off Calshot—and at Cowes that evening the weather was wretched, gloomy and cold and pouring with rain.

'I took my new friends to the yacht club to which I belonged and found it, as it not infrequently is, wholly deserted: not a soul there except the steward. But besides all this I knew perfectly well that where these gentlemen should be presented was the Royal Yacht Squadron. Out then into the rain.'

At the porter's lodge Scott Hughes explained his business to the signalman who, with an air of disbelief, listened before departing up the drive and into the Castle. Ten minutes later he returned and asked the party to follow him, which they did to the front door.

'When the door opened, bathing us in a warm glow of light, a man within, dressed in a steward's rig-out, asked who we were and what we wanted. Again I said that our boat was entered for the RYS regattas, that if they were available it would be helpful to receive a programme, and that, as these gentlemen were from abroad, it would be—er—well—nice if one or two other points could be made plain to them.

'The man withdrew. Withdrawn also was the warm glow of light, for he had closed the door. But quite shortly he reapp—but no! This was another man, and quite evidently a grade or so superior.

'"What was the name of the boat?"

'"*Noreg.*"

'"*Noreg? Noreg?* And the owner's name?"

'"Prince Olaf of Norway."

'Our interlocutor vanished.

'Two minutes later my new friends and I were on the Platform, as this famous room is misleadingly called, being successively introduced, for dinner was just over, to much the most charming men that we had ever met in all our lives.

'But, that this expression may have the stricter veracity, I ought rather to say that *I* was never so charmed in my life.'

Twice round, sir?

It is by no means certain that the protagonist of this story, related by John Scott Hughes, was aboard a Squadron yacht, but where else would such a faithful paid hand serve, and one so totally seeped in regatta racing?

After two very long, wet, windy days and two even longer, wet, windy nights, one of the smaller yachts in the 1928 Channel Race at last crossed the finishing line. As the gun fired the drenched and weary but indomitable hand turned to his owner and, in all good faith, shouted: 'Twice round, sir?'

What's in a name?

Captain John Illingworth, RN, a noted ocean racing yachtsman, was a Naval Member of the Squadron. It was Illingworth who, after the war when yachts were prohibitively expensive to build, introduced smaller and cheaper—and faster—designs. Some of them were not particularly elegant and in fact some, much to the disgust of some members, seemed downright ugly. One was called *Mouse of Malham*, and very successful she was, but it wasn't long before she was being known as the *Bat of Balham*.

Franglais

After the Second World War cruising remained popular among members, with France still the favourite destination. However, the postwar generation of members had perhaps not quite as much practice of speaking French as their predecessors. On one occasion this caused some confusion. The Household Brigade yacht *Gladeye*, with several members aboard, was approaching an unfamiliar French creek at dusk where the anchorage was known to be tricky. A French yacht lay anchored ahead, but in the half-light no one could see in which direction her anchor was lying. So as they passed, a member shouted '*Où est votre anchre, m'sieur?*' to a rather ancient Frenchman sitting in the cockpit.

The Frenchman cupped his ear. '*Quoi?*'

'*Où est votre anchre?*' the member repeated in his schoolboy French.

The old man shrugged, went below and then appeared once more with an even more elderly Frenchman.

'*Voici, mon oncle,*' he shouted, '*mais pourquoi?*'

Pour another tot

Ocean racing is a serious business nowadays, especially when it is the Fastnet Race, but during the 1950s it was tackled at a more leisurely—but still enthusiastic—pace. Alcohol was as necessary an ingredient in getting a yacht around the rugged rock as wind. This can be proved by the following conversation between some club members, as they struggled with sheets and sails in the Irish Sea while making sure they managed to down a morning bracer.

'Three inches out on the mainsheet.'
'Two inches in on the genoa.'
'Stop up the spinnaker.'
'Stop up the gin bottle.'

The age of austerity

In the period following the Second World War not many people had any money, and the few that did mostly chose not to flaunt it. Notable exceptions to this attitude were Sir Bernard and Lady Docker. Sir Bernard, let it be added, was never a member of the Squadron, yet his name has been perpetuated there by a distinguished yachtsman who is. As a young man during the late 1950s Michael Boyle owned not one but two 12 Metres. One morning his professional skipper came to the Castle and asked which of them he wanted to race that day. Boyle lowered his morning paper and said 'Both', before resuming his perusal of the news. From that moment he was affectionately known by his friends as 'Docker' Boyle.

No snogging 'ere

The Squadron lawn has always been a hallowed piece of turf, but Eros is no respecter of tradition. To celebrate the Queen's Jubilee in 1977 the Castle was thrown open to the public for the very first time. The charge was 50p, for a deserving charity. One fine afternoon the club's invaluable signalman spotted a couple on the grass engaged in what he later described as 'carrying on'. Horrified, he hurried away to tell the Secretary. The Secretary told the signalman to put a stop to it. The signalman suggested that this was the function of the Secretary, not the signalman, but the Secretary stood his ground. Reluctantly the signalman approached the couple and planted his feet firmly on the sacred grass. 'You can't do that there 'ere,' he said. The young man raised himself on one elbow and replied that as he had paid his 50p he could do what he effing well pleased. 'Oh, no you can't,' retorted the signalman. 'My members pays a hundred guineas a year and they're not allowed to.' He paused and then added, 'At least not in daytime they're not.'

Bingo!

Running the start line for Cowes Week, which is always done from the Squadron Platform, is a complicated business nowadays, but not even a modern computer can tell which yacht is finishing and when. So a line officer calls out a yacht's sail number as she crosses the line and her time is then tapped into the computer. This calling-out of numbers tends to confuse the public, who like watching the finish of a race standing on the battlements below the Platform. On one occasion a woman glanced up at the busy scene above her and, in all innocence, asked: 'Is that a bingo hall up there?'

Aspiring candidate

Said one witty member of an unfortunate yachts-man seeking election for the fourth time: 'I like him for his lack of pride.'